Underwater World / El mundo submarino

CLOWNFISH/ PECES PAYASO

By Ryan Nagelhout

Traducción al español: Eduardo Alamán

Please visit our website, www.garethstevens.com. For a free color catalog of all our high-quality books, call toll free 1-800-542-2595 or fax 1-877-542-2596.

Publisher Cataloging Data

Nagelhout, Ryan
[Clownfish. Spanish & English]
Clownfish = Peces payaso / by Ryan Nagelhout ; traducción al español, Eduardo Alamán.
p. cm. - (Underwater world = El mundo submarino)
Includes index.
Summary: Simple text and photographs tell about clownfish, including their habitat and how they stay safe from predators.
Contents: Meet the clownfish = Conoce al pez payaso - Home sweet home = Hogar, dulce hogar - Dangerous neighbors = Vecinos peligrosos.
ISBN 978-1-4339-8778-6
1. Anemonefishes—Juvenile literature [1. Anemonefishes 2. Spanish language materials—Bilingual] I. Title II. Title: Peces payaso

First Edition

Published in 2013 by
Gareth Stevens Publishing
111 East 14th Street, Suite 349
New York, NY 10003

Editor: Ryan Nagelhout
Designer: Katelyn Londino
Spanish Translation: Eduardo Alamán

Photo credits: Cover, pp. 1, 5, 7, 9 iStockphoto/Thinkstock.com; pp. 11, 13, 24 (sea) Rich Carey/Shutterstock.com; p. 15 © iStockphoto.com/parfyonov; pp. 17, 24 (reef) © iStockphoto.com/EXTREME-PHOTOGRAPHER; p. 19 Jeff Hunter/Photographer's Choice/Getty Images; pp. 21, 24 (anemone) Frank Wasserfuehrer/Shutterstock.com; p. 23 Willyam Bradberry/Shutterstock.com.

Printed in the United States of America

CPSIA compliance information: Batch #CW13GS: For further information contact Gareth Stevens, New York, New York at 1-800-542-2595.

Contents

Contenido

A clownfish has
three stripes.
It is often orange.

El pez payaso tiene
tres franjas.
Con frecuencia, son
de color naranja.

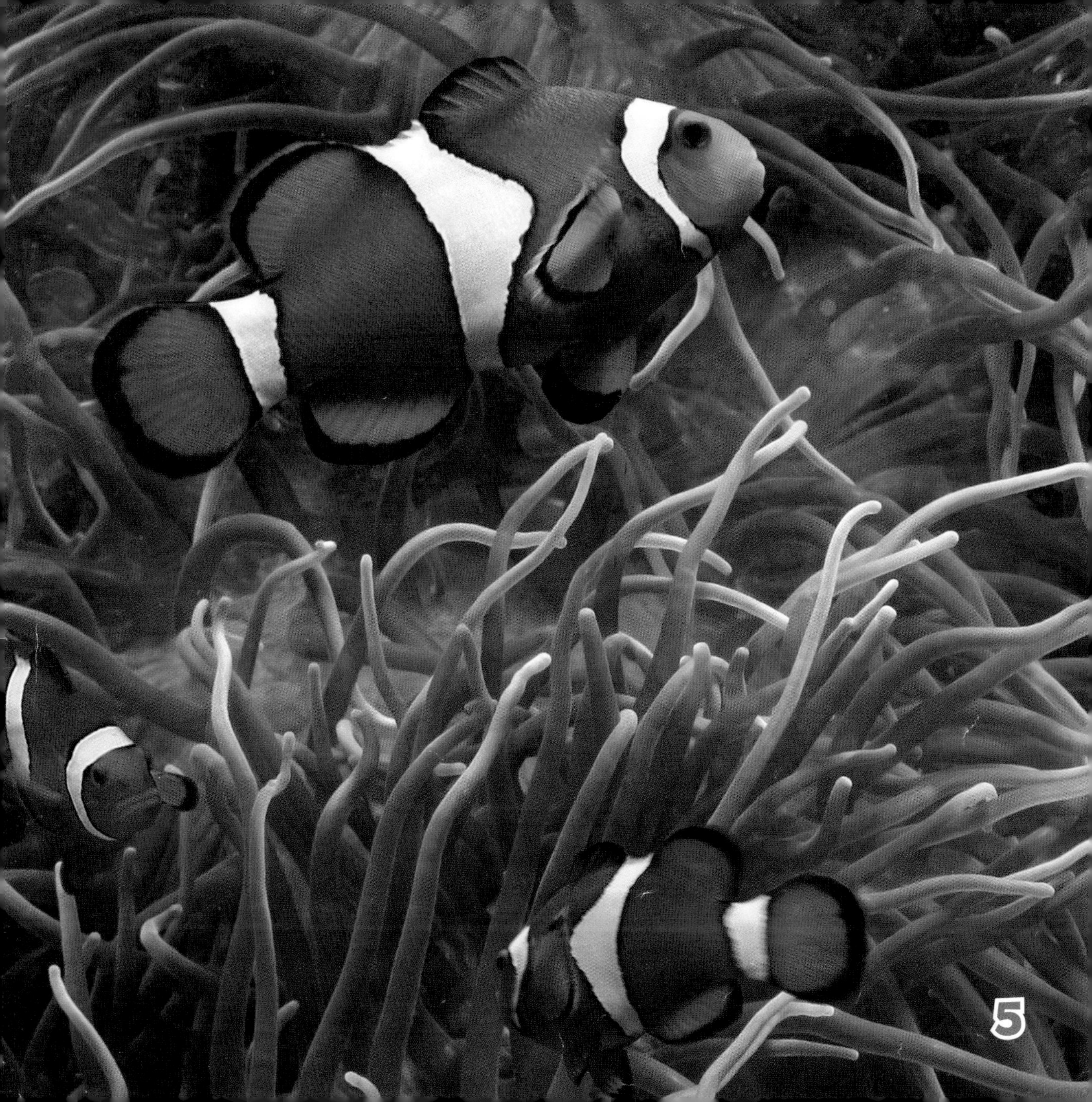

It can live
up to 10 years.

El pez payaso puede
vivir hasta 10 años.

There are over
27 kinds.

Hay más de 27 tipos
de pez payaso.

It lives in the sea.

El pez payaso vive
en el mar.

It likes to live
in warm water.

Al pez payaso le gusta
el agua templada.

It swims at the sea floor.

El pez payaso
nada cerca del
fondo del mar.

It swims around a reef.
This is its home.

El pez payaso nada
cerca del arrecife.
Esta es su casa.

Its bright colors can bring danger.

Sus colores brillantes pueden ser un peligro.

It stays near helpful animals to live. These are called anemones.

El pez payaso vive cerca de animales que lo ayudan. Estos se llaman anémonas.

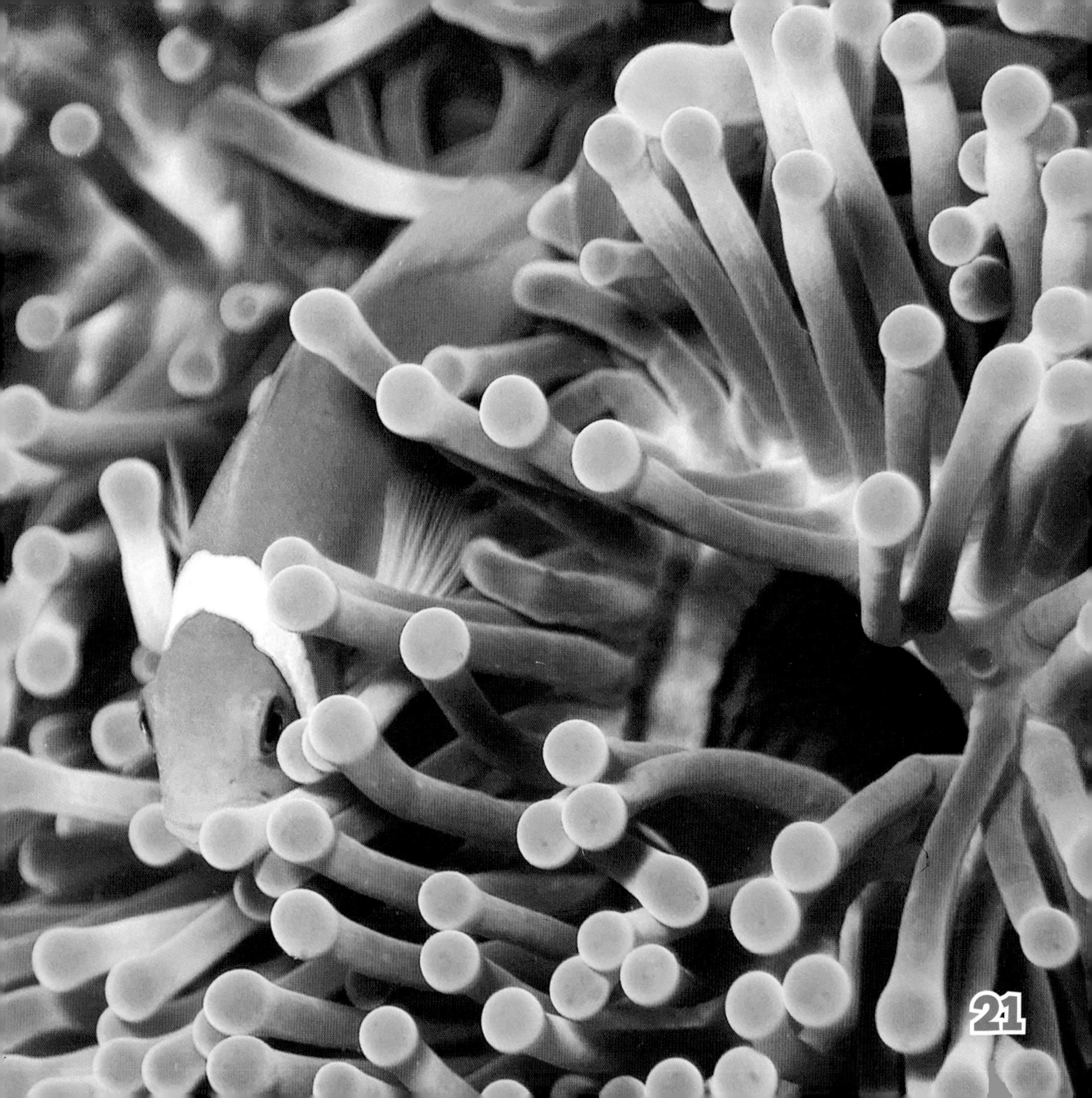

They work with each other to get food.

Trabajan en equipo para encontrar comida.

Words to Know/ Palabras que debes saber

anemone/
(las) anémonas

reef/
(el) arrecife

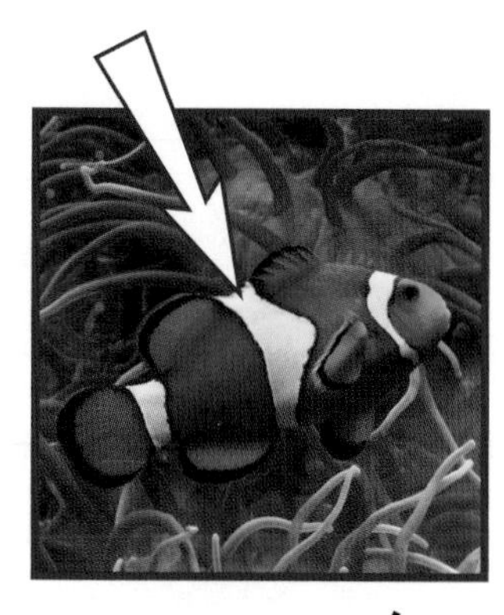
stripe/
(la) franja

Index / Índice